THE REAL COCKTAIL BOOK

Modern & Classic Cocktail Recipes For Every Occasion

1st Edition

George Jacob Smith

ISBN- 9781099446085

TABLE OF CONTENTS

3

DISCLAIMER

I think it's time for a cocktail! Do you want to meet up for a few cocktails before the show? The cocktail is a permanent fixture in modern society, but where did the idea come from? What even is a cocktail? And what about the cocktail party, who was the genius that created this event and why was it invented? As you begin your foray into the world of mixology maybe these are some questions you find popping into your head while you try to figure out what a dash or splash of something is or what the heck it means to muddle that herb.

So, what is a cocktail? And when did it become a thing?

Originally the concoctions we now call cocktails went by the name "slings" which heralded from the German word "schlingen." This word literally translates to swallow quickly. The "slings" of old were a simple a liquor mixed with water, a sweetener of some sort and bitters. Probably why the people who partook of these beverages wanted to swallow quickly. Though in truth classic cocktails like the Old-Fashioned pretty much stick with this recipe the refining process of liquor and the multitudes of options for sweeteners have improved vastly since the birth of the cocktail.

The rebranding of the "sling" into the cocktail happened sometime in the late 1700's or early 1800s depending n which piece of history you subscribe to. In the U.S. the term shows up first in 1803 in "The Farmers' Cabinet". The variation of the term does show up in the U.K. earlier than that but doesn't get defined until 1806. When in a publication it is defined in the recipe mentioned above.

In modern society, the definition of a cocktail is not nearly as narrow as that one. Today, when we talk about grabbing a cocktail, is simply meant we are going to drink any number of mixed drink concoctions that now live on the menu of the millions of bars around the world. Though professional bartender will know the difference and still consider a cocktail in its original form many of us civilians stick to our guns and what we know. Whatever you call these alcoholic concoctions they rea great to sip on while relaxing after a long day of work or at that co-worker's cocktail party you didn't really want to attend.

Speaking of that cocktail party, who came up with that gem of an idea? A party before dinner? Whoever they are they should be given some sort of award.

Everyone loves a good cocktail party and it would make sense that many people want to lay claim to the invention, but who is the true genius? The earliest mention is usually the correct choice, and, in that case, the first mention of a cocktail party is found in a newspaper article from 1917. This article names a St. Louis woman as the mother of this invention. Her name was Mrs. Clara Bell Walsh and she was the first reported person to hold a party solely devoted to mixed drinks. Her invention was out of necessity as the temperance movement was growing in popularity the bars and places the people would normally retire to get their drink on as it was drying up. So, the people that wanted to partake of the spirits had to find a new place to do that and where better than from the comfort of their own homes or at the least one of their friends. So, let's all say a big thank you to our sister suffragette and continue to honor her by throwing our own cocktail parties.

Now those burning questions answered let's get down to some other important questions you might have.

Like what do I need to have to craft that perfect cocktail? Or what does this weird bar lingo mean?

TOOLS OF THE TRADE

When you build a house, you have a tools box and trying your hand at being a mixologist is no different. Here are some essentials you may want to have in your toolbox:

SHAKER:

Though there are many styles of the shaker as a new cocktail crafter you just need the basics. For this, you have a choice of either a Cobbler or a Boston Shaker. The cobbler is the better for a novice cocktail craftsperson.

STRAINER:

Many cocktails call for muddling and if you want a smooth cocktail in the glass then a strainer is a must-have for every home bar. Though the Cobbler shaker comes with a built-in a strainer if you opted for any other type this is something you will want to buy. Plus having an extra never hurts.

JIGGER:

Cocktails are a fine science and just a drop too much of one of the ingredients can ruin the whole thing. So measuring is important, and the jigger is what bartenders use to measure their drinks out. Unless you want to fee pour and then you are taking your own reputation in your hands.

COCKTAIL SPOON:

A cocktail spoon is a uniquely designed utensil. It has a long handle that is spiraled to help when creating layered cocktails. The cocktail spoon is a definite must as it fits in any glass and a because of the long handle can also be used to stir drinks while still in the cocktail shaker.

CITRUS JUICER:

This is a tool many kitchens already have in them. The juicer will make sure that when juicing that lemon or lime for the fresh juice required you get every drop you need.

MUDDLER:

You may have seen this it looks kind of like a little bat. The muddler is important for crafting cocktails like the Mojito to bruise the mint. By bruising the mint your release all the oils and aroma from the herb thereby infusing your cocktail with its essence.

CHANNEL KNIFE:

Want to add those pretty citrus peel flourishes? Then the channel knife is something you should have in your bars tool kit. This small spoon-shaped knife can peel long thin fruit peels that will elevate your cocktail game.

GLASSES:

There are so many styles of glasses that it could take you a long time to collect. Some must have for the beginning bar are Collins, Old Fashioned, Martini and Coup glasses. Starting with these will get you started on the right foot.

SOME THINGS YOU SHOULD KNOW

There are some lingo and stuff that would help to know when beginning your cocktail journey. Make sure you know these:

MIXERS:

Non-alcoholic ingredients that are added to mixed drinks. This can include syrups, bitters, sodas, etc.

GARNISH:

A decoration used at the end of crafting your cocktail to give it a flourish. Common garnishes are fruits or even herbs and are often things used in the cocktail itself.

SIMPLE SYRUP:

A sweetener used any many cocktails.

Recipe:

1. Pour equal parts of water and sugar into a pot.
2. Heat over low heat until the sugar is fully dissolved.
3. Take off the heat and if you want to add flavor add your chosen one now.
4. Once completely cool remove flavoring if you added it.
5. Keep it cold and use as needed.

With every cocktail, you can make it your own by changing just one or two things in the recipe. Here are some ideas to craft a uniquely your cocktail.

MIXING IT UP:

- Mixers: If you're feeling a little adventurous change up your mixers.

- Bitters: There is a world of new craft bitters, so to change the flavor profile try a different bitter or even add a bitter to a cocktail that doesn't call for one.

- Fruits & Juices: Try a different fruit or juice combination to add a little difference to the traditional cocktail recipes.

- Alcohols: You can always change the alcohol you are using or simply try an infused variety of the one the recipe calls for.

- Smoke: Add a smoky flavor by grilling the fruit in your recipe. Or literally, smoke your cocktail. Smoking is not just for meat and can add a unique twist to your cocktail.

- Heat: If you can't stand the heat. No really a great way tweak your cocktail recipe is by adding a heating element. Whether it is spicy or just warming you can try adding herbs like cinnamon or nutmeg. Or you can just slap a jalapeno or whatever pepper you are thinking will light the place up.

- Herbs & Spices: You can add or switch out the herb or spice element in your cocktail. Even try floral notes like lavender or violet for a trendier vibe.

- Bubbles: Even if your cocktail recipe doesn't call for it you can add in a bubble element. Try adding ginger beer or sparkling water to add some effervescence.

- Salts & Sugars: You can switch up your sugar source. Use honey or agave instead of sugar. Another fun thing you can do is add a rim of salt or sugar to your cocktail to change it up. Shoot infuse your salt or sugar with herbs or spices like vanilla, lavender or even chili's.

- Seasons: Switch the fruit and spice notes out for a seasonal touch. If in autumn, try an apple cinnamon flavor profile and if in summer try lemon and lavender.

You are now armed with a basic knowledge of the cocktail and can begin to craft some classic, soon to be classics and your own unique adult beverages. All that is left is for you to whip up some killer cocktails and then get that party started. Try some of these awesome cocktail recipes and wow your friends and family with your mixologist skills.

VODKA

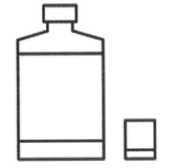

INGREDIENTS:

- ♦ 2 oz. vodka
- ♦ 5 oz. tomato juice
- ♦ 5 tsp. prepared horseradish
- ♦ 3 dashes hot sauce
- ♦ 2-3 dashes of Worcestershire sauce
- ♦ 2 lime wedges
- ♦ Lemon wedge
- ♦ Celery salt
- ♦ Black pepper
- ♦ Celery stalk for garnish

NUTRITIONAL FACTS:

- ♦ Net Carb: 6.8g
- ♦ Fiber: .8g
- ♦ Fat: 0g
- ♦ Protein: 1.2g
- ♦ Kcal: 125

CRAFTING THE COCKTAIL:

1. In a shaker, squeeze lemon and lime wedge over ice.

2. Add all the remaining ingredients to the shaker and shake.

3. Pour the liquid over ice in a tall glass. Garnish with a celery stalk and another lime wedge.

INGREDIENTS:

- ♦ 2 oz. vodka
- ♦ 4 oz. cranberry juice
- ♦ 0.5 oz. lime juice
- ♦ Lime wedge to garnish

NUTRITIONAL FACTS:

- ♦ Net Carb: 18
- ♦ Fiber: .1g
- ♦ Fat: .2g
- ♦ Protein: .6g
- ♦ Kcal: 131

CRAFTING THE COCKTAIL:

1. Put ice in a highball glass.

2. Add vodka and juices to the glass.

3. Garnish with the lime wedge.

INGREDIENTS:

- ◆ 1.5 oz. vodka
- ◆ 3.5 oz. grapefruit juice
- ◆ Kosher salt
- ◆ Lime wedge
- ◆ A handful of basil
- ◆ Dash of orange bitters
- ◆ Simple Syrup (*recipe under Techniques)

NUTRITIONAL FACTS:

- ◆ Net Carb: 14.1g
- ◆ Fiber: .2g
- ◆ Fat: .2g
- ◆ Protein: 1g
- ◆ Kcal: 157

CRAFTING THE COCKTAIL:

1. Muddle basil in a glass.

2. Pour kosher salt onto a plate.

3. Moisten the glass rim with a split lime wedge and gently coat the rim of the glass with salt.

4. Add the ice, dash of orange bitters, vodka, simple syrup, and grapefruit juice.

INGREDIENTS:

- ♦ 1.5 oz. vodka
- ♦ .5 oz. cranberry juice
- ♦ .25 oz. simple syrup
- ♦ .25 oz. lime juice
- ♦ Lime wedge to garnish

NUTRITIONAL FACTS:

- ♦ Net Carb: 13g
- ♦ Fiber: .1g
- ♦ Fat: 0g
- ♦ Protein: .1g
- ♦ Kcal: 213

CRAFTING THE COCKTAIL:

1. Place all ingredients in a shaker and add ice.

2. Shake well and strain the liquid into a cocktail or martini glass.

3. Garnish with the lime peel or wedge.

INGREDIENTS:

- ◆ 2 oz. vodka
- ◆ 1 oz Galliano liqueur
- ◆ 5 oz. orange juice
- ◆ Cherry for garnish
- ◆ Orange slice for garnish

NUTRITIONAL FACTS:

- ◆ Net Carb: 11g
- ◆ Fiber: 0g
- ◆ Fat: 0g
- ◆ Protein: 0g
- ◆ Kcal: 250

CRAFTING THE COCKTAIL:

1. Put ice in a highball glass.

2. Mix vodka and orange juice together in the glass.

3. Top off with Galliano.

4. Garnish with cherry and orange slice.

INGREDIENTS:

- ◆ 1 oz. vodka
- ◆ .25 oz. orange liqueur
- ◆ .25 oz. lime juice

NUTRITIONAL FACTS:

- ◆ Net Carb: 7.8g
- ◆ Fiber: .1g
- ◆ Fat: 0g
- ◆ Protein: .1g
- ◆ Kcal: 174

CRAFTING THE COCKTAIL:

1. Combine ingredients with is in a shaker.

2. Shake and strain the liquid into either a shot glass or martini glass.

INGREDIENTS:

- ♦ 3 oz. vodka
- ♦ 1 oz. dry vermouth
- ♦ Lemon peel

NUTRITIONAL FACTS:

- ♦ Net Carb: 4g
- ♦ Fiber: .3g
- ♦ Fat: 1g
- ♦ Protein: .1g
- ♦ Kcal: 250

CRAFTING THE COCKTAIL:

1. Combine all ingredients into a cocktail shaker, but do not shake. Add ice and stir.

2. Strain liquid into a cocktail or martini glass. Garnish with a lemon twist.

3. If you want to make it a dirty Martini add a splash of olive brine and two olives.

INGREDIENTS:

- 3 slices of ginger
- 1 ½ tsp. superfine sugar
- 5 sprigs mint
- 4 oz. vodka
- Ice

NUTRITIONAL FACTS:

- Net Carb: 8.7g
- Fiber: 1g
- Fat: 0g
- Protein: .3g
- Kcal: 161

CRAFTING THE COCKTAIL:

1. Muddle the ginger and sugar together in a glass.
2. Add mint sprigs and muddle until fragrant.
3. Add the vodka and some ice.
4. Stir.
5. Garnish with mint.

INGREDIENTS:

- ◆ 1 oz. vodka
- ◆ .5 oz. lavender infused simple syrup
- ◆ .5 oz. lemon juice
- ◆ .5 oz Mandarin/tangerine puree
- ◆ 2 dashes of cardamom bitters
- ◆ Soda to top
- ◆ Mint leaves to garnish

NUTRITIONAL FACTS:

- ◆ Net Carb: 29.2g
- ◆ Fiber: 0g
- ◆ Fat: 0g
- ◆ Protein: 1g
- ◆ Kcal: 194

CRAFTING THE COCKTAIL:

1. Place all ingredients in a shaker and shake very well.

2. Pour (do not strain) into a cocktail or martini glass.

3. Top glass with club soda. Garnish with mint leaves.

INGREDIENTS:

- ◆ 1 – 1 ½ oz. vodka
- ◆ 1 oz. Kahlua
- ◆ 2 oz. cream
- ◆ 1 tbs. caramel sauce
- ◆ Course sea salt for garnish

NUTRITIONAL FACTS:

- ◆ Net Carb: 69.5g
- ◆ Fiber: 0g
- ◆ Fat: 12g
- ◆ Protein: 2.3g
- ◆ Kcal: 224

CRAFTING THE COCKTAIL:

1. Put ice, the Kahlua, vodka, cream, and ½ tablespoon of the caramel in a shaker.

2. Shake well.

3. Use the rest of the caramel sauce to rim a cocktail or martini glass.

4. Fill glass with ice and pour the mixture on top.

5. Use the course sea salt to garnish (you may also put it on the rim with the caramel sauce).

INGREDIENTS:

- ◆ 1 jalapeño
- ◆ 2 oz. vodka
- ◆ 4 oz. ginger beer
- ◆ 1 oz. lime juice
- ◆ .5 oz. orange liqueur

NUTRITIONAL FACTS:

- ◆ Net Carb: 13.4g
- ◆ Fiber: 0g
- ◆ Fat: 0g
- ◆ Protein: 0 g
- ◆ Protein: 0g
- ◆ Kcal: 180

CRAFTING THE COCKTAIL:

1. Thinly slice the jalapeño and muddle a few slices with the orange liqueur and lime juice liqueur in a copper mug or Collins glass.

2. Stir in the vodka and ginger beer and add some ice.

3. Garnish with a slice or two of the jalapeños and serve.

INGREDIENTS:

- ◆ 1.5 oz. vodka
- ◆ .75 oz. lemon juice
- ◆ .25 oz Crème de Cacao
- ◆ .25 oz spiced pear liqueur
- ◆ .125 oz. maple syrup
- ◆ 1 dash of chocolate bitters
- ◆ Lemon peel
- ◆ Ice

NUTRITIONAL FACTS:

- ◆ Net Carb: 8.3g
- ◆ Fiber: 0g
- ◆ Fat: 0g
- ◆ Protein: 0g
- ◆ Kcal: 241

CRAFTING THE COCKTAIL:

1. Place all the ingredients in a cocktail shaker with some ice.

2. Shake well.

3. Pour into a cocktail glass and garnish with a lemon twist.

GIN

INGREDIENTS:

- ◆ 2 oz. gin
- ◆ .25 oz. lemon juice
- ◆ Agave nectar
- ◆ Sparkling apple cider
- ◆ Garnished with thyme and apple

NUTRITIONAL FACTS:

- ◆ Net Carb: 46.5g
- ◆ Fiber: 0g
- ◆ Fat: 0g
- ◆ Protein: 1g
- ◆ Kcal: 332

CRAFTING THE COCKTAIL:

1. Pour gin into a shaker.
2. Add the agave nectar and lemon juice.
3. Shake well and pour in a highball glass.
4. Top with sparkling cider.
5. Garnish with an apple slice and some fresh thyme.

INGREDIENTS:

- ◆ 2.5 oz. gin
- ◆ 1 oz. lemon juice
- ◆ .5 oz blueberry puree or blueberry grenadine
- ◆ Blueberries to garnish
- ◆ Lemon slices to garnish
- ◆ Selzer to top

NUTRITIONAL FACTS:

- ◆ Net Carb: 90.6g
- ◆ Fiber: .2g
- ◆ Fat: .1g
- ◆ Protein: .2g
- ◆ Kcal: 497

CRAFTING THE COCKTAIL:

1. Add all ingredients to a shaker, excluding the seltzer.
2. Shake and strain into a stemless wine glass with some ice.
3. Top off with seltzer
4. Garnish with lemon slices and blueberries.

INGREDIENTS:

- ◆ 1.5 oz. gin
- ◆ 1 oz. simple syrup
- ◆ .75 oz. lemon juice
- ◆ 2 dashes Angostura bitters
- ◆ Lemon peel
- ◆ Ice

NUTRITIONAL FACTS:

- ◆ Net Carb: 10g
- ◆ Fiber: .1g
- ◆ Fat: 0g
- ◆ Protein: .1g
- ◆ Kcal: 213

CRAFTING THE COCKTAIL:

1. Combine all ingredients in a cocktail shaker with some ice and shake.

2. Strain liquid into an old-fashioned glass filled with ice.

3. Garnish with lemon peel.

INGREDIENTS:

- ♦ 1 ½ oz. gin
- ♦ ½ oz lime juice
- ♦ ½ oz. Crème de Framboise liqueur
- ♦ 4 oz. ginger ale
- ♦ Lime wedge
- ♦ Ice

NUTRITIONAL FACTS:

- ♦ Net Carb: 24g
- ♦ Fiber: 2g
- ♦ Fat: 0g
- ♦ Protein: 0g
- ♦ Kcal: 218

CRAFTING THE COCKTAIL:

1. Fill a highball glass with ice.
2. Pour the lime juice, gin, and Crème de Framboise into a high ball glass.
3. Top glass with the ginger ale.
4. Garnish with a lime wedge.

INGREDIENTS:

- ◆ 2 oz. gin
- ◆ ¾oz. fresh lime juice
- ◆ ¾ oz. simple syrup
- ◆ Cucumber wheel or lime wedge for garnish
- ◆ Ice

NUTRITIONAL FACTS:

- ◆ Net Carb: 11g
- ◆ Fiber: .1g
- ◆ Fat: 0g
- ◆ Protein: .1g
- ◆ Kcal: 223

CRAFTING THE COCKTAIL:

1. Fill shaker with ice and pourgin, lime juice, and simple syrup into the shaker.

2. Stir vigorously with a long cocktail spoon until very cold.

3. Strain into a chilled martini glass.

4. Garnish with a cucumber wheel or lime wedge and serve.

INGREDIENTS:

- ◆ 2 oz. dry gin
- ◆ 1 oz. yellow chartreuse
- ◆ .5 oz. lime juice
- ◆ .5 oz. lemon juice
- ◆ .75 oz. tarragon tea syrup (see below)
- ◆ Tarragon leaves for garnish
- ◆ Ice

NUTRITIONAL FACTS:

- ◆ Net Carb: 21.6g
- ◆ Fiber: 0g
- ◆ Fat: 0g
- ◆ Protein: .5g
- ◆ Kcal: 299

CRAFTING THE COCKTAIL:

1. To make Tarragon tea syrup:

2. Ina pot, mix 2 cups of water, ½ cup of sugar, and ½ cup of tarragon. Boil and remove from heat. Allow to cool before using in cocktails.

3. Place all ingredients in a cocktail shaker with ice but do not shake. Stir together.

4. Strain into a cocktail or martini glass.

5. Garnish with tarragon leaves.

INGREDIENTS:

- ◆ 1.5 oz. gin
- ◆ .5 oz. lemon juice
- ◆ .25 Lavender simple syrup
- ◆ Ice
- ◆ Lemon wheels
- ◆ Lavender Sprigs

NUTRITIONAL FACTS:

- ◆ Net Carb: 24g
- ◆ Fiber: 0g
- ◆ Fat: 0g
- ◆ Protein: 0g
- ◆ Kcal: 202

CRAFTING THE COCKTAIL:

1. Combine ice and ingredients in a shaker.

2. Shake and pour into coup glasses.

3. Garnish with a sprig of lavender and a lemon wheel.

INGREDIENTS:

- ◆ 1 oz. gin
- ◆ 1 oz. Campari
- ◆ 1 oz. sweet vermouth
- ◆ Orange twist to garnish
- ◆ Ice

NUTRITIONAL FACTS:

- ◆ Net Carb: 12g
- ◆ Fiber: 0g
- ◆ Fat: 0g
- ◆ Protein: .1g
- ◆ Kcal: 200

CRAFTING THE COCKTAIL:

1. Combine gin, Campari, and sweet vermouth in a shaker.

2. Stir until combined and strain into an old-fashioned glass with a single large ice cube.

3. Garnish with the orange twist.

INGREDIENTS:

- .75 oz. dry gin
- .25 oz. Cherry liqueur
- .25 oz. Grand Marnier
- .25 oz. herbal liqueur
- 1 oz. pineapple juice
- .5 oz. lime juice
- 1 dash of bitters
- Club soda
- Ice
- Orange lice to garnish
- Cherry to garnish

NUTRITIONAL FACTS:

- Net Carb: 12.1g
- Fiber: 0g
- Fat: .1g
- Protein: .1g
- Kcal: 229

CRAFTING THE COCKTAIL:

1. Place all the ingredients except for the club soda in a shaker with ice.

2. Shake and strain the liquid into a highball glass.

3. Top glass with the club soda.

4. Garnish with a cherry and an orange slice.

INGREDIENTS:

- ◆ .75 oz. lemon juice
- ◆ .25 oz Suze
- ◆ .5 oz. Bigallet China China
- ◆ .75 oz. cherry liqueur
- ◆ .75 oz. gin
- ◆ Lemon wheel for garnish
- ◆ Thyme sprig for garnish

NUTRITIONAL FACTS:

- ◆ Net Carb: 7.3g
- ◆ Fiber: 0g
- ◆ Fat: 0g
- ◆ Protein: 0g
- ◆ Kcal: 173

CRAFTING THE COCKTAIL:

1. Place ice in a Collins glass to chill.

2. Combine the lemon juice, Suze, cherry liqueur, gin, and Bigallet China China in a cocktail shaker.

3. Shake and pour into the chilled Collins glass.

4. Top glass with club soda.

5. Garnish with sprig of thyme and a lemon wheel.

INGREDIENTS:

- ◆ 1 dash of orange bitters
- ◆ .5 oz. simple syrup
- ◆ .75 oz. fresh lemon juice
- ◆ 2 oz. gin
- ◆ Seltzer
- ◆ Lemon wedge for garnish
- ◆ Ice

NUTRITIONAL FACTS:

- ◆ Net Carb: 8.2g
- ◆ Fiber: .3g
- ◆ Fat: .1g
- ◆ Protein: .1g
- ◆ Kcal: 177

CRAFTING THE COCKTAIL:

1. Fill a cocktail shaker with ice and add the simple syrup, orange bitters, lemon juice, and gin.

2. Shake briefly until chilled.

3. Strain liquid into a Collins glass filled with ice.

4. Top with seltzer and garnish with lemon wedge.

INGREDIENTS:

- ◆ 2 Kaffir lime leaf
- ◆ .5 oz. fresh lemon juice
- ◆ .5 oz. ginger
- ◆ .5 oz. Giffard lychee
- ◆ 1 oz. Dolin Blanc
- ◆ 1 oz. gin
- ◆ Ice

NUTRITIONAL FACTS:

- ◆ Net Carb: 28.4g
- ◆ Fiber: .1g
- ◆ Fat: .1g
- ◆ Protein: .1g
- ◆ Kcal: 205

CRAFTING THE COCKTAIL:

1. Muddle the Kaffir lime leaf in a shaker and add ice.
2. Combine the ingredients into the shaker and stir with a long cocktail spoon.
3. Strain the liquid into a coup glass.
4. Garnish with a Kaffir lime leaf.

RUM

INGREDIENTS:

♦ 2 oz. Bacardi 8 Anos rum

♦ 1 tsp. sugar

♦ 2 dashes of Angostura bitters

♦ .5 oz. water

♦ Orange peel to garnish

♦ Ice

NUTRITIONAL FACTS:

♦ Net Carb: 6.7g

♦ Fiber: .2g

♦ Fat: 0g

♦ Protein: 0g

♦ Kcal: 176

CRAFTING THE COCKTAIL:

1. Pour the water, and bitters into an old-fashioned glass.

2. Combine with a cocktail spoon.

3. Add the rum.

4. Fill glass ¾ full with ice cubes and stir well.

5. Top with fresh ice.

6. Cut a wedge of orange and squeeze the juice over the cocktail.

7. Garnish with the orange peel.

INGREDIENTS:

- ♦ 2 oz. aged rum
- ♦ .5 oz. ginger simple syrup
- ♦ .5 oz. pineapple juice
- ♦ .5 oz. fresh lime juice
- ♦ 2 dashes Angostura bitters
- ♦ Soda water
- ♦ Lime wheels for garnish
- ♦ Ginger candy for garnish
- ♦ Ice

NUTRITIONAL FACTS:

- ♦ Net Carb: 13g
- ♦ Fiber: 0g
- ♦ Fat: 0g
- ♦ Protein: .1g
- ♦ Kcal: 183

CRAFTING THE COCKTAIL:

1. Add all ingredients to a cocktail shaker.
2. Shake and strain the liquid into a rocks glass filled with ice.
3. Top with soda
4. Garnish with ginger candy and a lime wheel.

INGREDIENTS:

- ◆ 2 oz. rum
- ◆ 4-5 oz. ginger beer
- ◆ Lime to garnish
- ◆ Ice

NUTRITIONAL FACTS:

- ◆ Net Carb: 11g
- ◆ Fiber: 0g
- ◆ Fat: 0g
- ◆ Protein: 0g
- ◆ Kcal: 170

CRAFTING THE COCKTAIL:

1. Fill a Collins glass with ice.
2. Pour in both the ginger beer and rum.
3. Stir well.
4. Garnish with lime.

INGREDIENTS:

- ◆ 4 oz. aged rum
- ◆ 1 oz. fresh lemon juice
- ◆ 2 oz. passion fruit syrup
- ◆ 1 oz. pineapple juice
- ◆ 1 tsp. grenadine
- ◆ 1 tsp simple syrup
- ◆ Orange slice to garnish
- ◆ Cherry to garnish
- ◆ Ice

NUTRITIONAL FACTS:

- ◆ Net Carb: 32g
- ◆ Fiber: 0g
- ◆ Fat: 0g
- ◆ Protein: 1g
- ◆ Kcal: 339

CRAFTING THE COCKTAIL:

1. Fill shaker 2/3 of the way with ice and add ingredients.
2. Shake well and then pour in a hurricane glass.
3. Add more ice as needed.
4. Garnish with a cherry and an orange slice.

INGREDIENTS:

- ♦ 2 oz. rum
- ♦ 2 oz. snap pea juice
- ♦ 1 oz. lime juice
- ♦ .5 oz. jasmine simple syrup
- ♦ Pea shoots and flower to garnish
- ♦ Ice

NUTRITIONAL FACTS:

- ♦ Net Carb: 10.9g
- ♦ Fiber: .8g
- ♦ Fat: 0g
- ♦ Protein: 8g
- ♦ Kcal: 172

CRAFTING THE COCKTAIL:

1. Combine all ingredients in a cocktail shaker.
2. Shake and strain the liquid into a highball glass filled with ice.
3. Garnish with flowers and pea shoots.

INGREDIENTS:

- ♦ 2 oz. rum
- ♦ 1 oz. fresh lime juice
- ♦ .5 oz. Cointreau
- ♦ .25 oz. walnut syrup
- ♦ Lime to garnish
- ♦ Mint to garnish
- ♦ Ice

NUTRITIONAL FACTS:

- ♦ Net Carb: 24g
- ♦ Fiber: .4g
- ♦ Fat: .2g
- ♦ Protein: .8g
- ♦ Kcal: 292

CRAFTING THE COCKTAIL:

1. Combine all ingredients in a cocktail shaker.
2. Shake and pour into Collins glass over crushed ice.
3. Garnish with mint and lime.

INGREDIENTS:

- 1 oz. rum
- 2 mints sprigs
- 1 tbsp. fresh lime juice
- ½ tsp sugar
- Club soda
- Lime for garnish
- Ice

NUTRITIONAL FACTS:

- Net Carb: 29g
- Fiber: 1.2g
- Fat: .1g
- Protein: .3g
- Kcal: 205

CRAFTING THE COCKTAIL:

1. Fill the shaker halfway with ice and add ingredients.
2. Shake and pour in a highball glass with ice.
3. Top off the drink with club soda.
4. Garnish with lime.

INGREDIENTS:

- ◆ 1.5 oz. rum
- ◆ .5 oz. pineapple rum
- ◆ .1 oz fresh lime juice
- ◆ 2 tsp. sugar or .75 oz. simple syrup
- ◆ Strawberry for muddling and garnish
- ◆ Ice

NUTRITIONAL FACTS:

- ◆ Net Carb: 13.8g
- ◆ Fiber: 0g
- ◆ Fat: 0g
- ◆ Protein: 0g
- ◆ Kcal: 170g

CRAFTING THE COCKTAIL:

1. Add a strawberry to shaker and muddle.
2. Combine all ingredients in the shaker and shake well.
3. Double strain the shaker into a Nick & Nora glass.
4. Garnish with strawberry.

INGREDIENTS:

- ◆ 1.5 oz. rum
- ◆ .5 oz. fresh lime juice
- ◆ .75 oz. simple syrup
- ◆ Lime wedges for garnish
- ◆ Raspberries to muddle and garnish
- ◆ Ice

NUTRITIONAL FACTS:

- ◆ Net Carb: 16.6g
- ◆ Fiber: 2.1g
- ◆ Fat: .2g
- ◆ Protein: 1g
- ◆ Kcal: 150

CRAFTING THE COCKTAIL:

1. Muddle raspberries in a shaker with lime juice.

2. Add ice and all remaining ingredients (besides lime wedge) into a cocktail shaker.

3. Shake well and strain liquid into a glass of ice.

4. Garnish with the lime wedge and raspberries.

INGREDIENTS:

- ◆ 2 oz. rum
- ◆ 1 oz. fresh grapefruit juice
- ◆ .5 oz. fresh lime juice
- ◆ 1 oz. Grenadine
- ◆ 1 tbsp. sugar cane syrup
- ◆ .5 oz. 151 rum (optional)
- ◆ Ice

NUTRITIONAL FACTS:

- ◆ Net Carb: 37g
- ◆ Fiber: 1g
- ◆ Fat: .3g
- ◆ Protein: 1.3g
- ◆ Kcal: 347

CRAFTING THE COCKTAIL:

1. Add ice and all ingredients (except 151) to a shaker.

2. Shake and strain liquid into a Collins glass filled with ice.

3. Top off with 151 rum.

INGREDIENT:

- ◆ 2 oz. aged rum
- ◆ Dash of ground cinnamon
- ◆ .25 oz. orange juice
- ◆ .25 oz. fresh lemon juice
- ◆ .5 oz simple syrup
- ◆ Candied ginger for garnish
- ◆ Ice

NUTRITIONAL FACTS:

- ◆ Net Carb: 12.2g
- ◆ Fiber: 0g
- ◆ Fat: 0g
- ◆ Protein: .2g
- ◆ Kcal: 147

CRAFTING THE COCKTAIL:

1. Combine all ingredients in a cocktail shaker.
2. Shake well and strain over ice into a rocks glass.
3. Garnish with the candied ginger.

INGREDIENTS:

- ◆ 1 oz. light rum
- ◆ 1 oz. dark rum
- ◆ 1 oz. orange liqueur
- ◆ .5 oz. fresh lemon juice
- ◆ .5 oz. fresh lime juice
- ◆ 1.5 oz. orange juice
- ◆ 1.5 oz. passion fruit puree or syrup
- ◆ .25 oz. Grenadine
- ◆ 2 dashes of Angostura bitters
- ◆ .5 oz. 151 rum (optional)
- ◆ Mint for garnish
- ◆ Seasonal fruit for garnish

NUTRITIONAL FACTS:

- ◆ Net Carb: 13g
- ◆ Fiber: .2g
- ◆ Fat: .1g
- ◆ Protein: .1g
- ◆ Kcal: 371

CRAFTING THE COCKTAIL:

1. Combine all the ingredients in a cocktail shaker with ice.
2. Shake well and strain into a large glass filled with ice.
3. Top with 151 rum if you choose to.
4. Garnish with fruit and mint.

WHISKEY

INGREDIENTS:

- ♦ 1.5 oz. rye whiskey
- ♦ .75 oz. dry vermouth
- ♦ .75 oz. pineapple juice

NUTRITIONAL FACTS:

- ♦ Net Carb: 9.5g
- ♦ Fiber: .1g
- ♦ Fat: 0g
- ♦ Protein: .2g
- ♦ Kcal: 210

CRAFTING THE COCKTAIL:

1. Combine ice and ingredients in a shaker.
2. Shake and strain liquid into a chilled cocktail glass.

INGREDIENTS:

- ♦ 2 oz. whiskey
- ♦ .75 oz agave or honey syrup
- ♦ 4 oz. blood orange juice
- ♦ ½ small jalapeño
- ♦ Blood orange slices to garnish
- ♦ Half of the jalapeño to garnish (optional)
- ♦ Ice

NUTRITIONAL FACTS:

- ♦ Net Carb: 26g
- ♦ Fiber: 1.5g
- ♦ Fat: 0g
- ♦ Protein: .5g
- ♦ Kcal: 234

CRAFTING THE COCKTAIL:

1. Combine ice, whiskey, syrup, juice and chopped jalapeño in a shaker.

2. Shake well and strain over ice into a rocks glass.

3. Garnish with blood orange slice and jalapeño (optional).

INGREDIENTS:

- ◆ 3 oz. Irish Whiskey
- ◆ 1 oz. Grenadine
- ◆ 5-6 oz. Sprite or ginger ale
- ◆ .25 oz of fresh lemon juice
- ◆ .25 oz. lime juice
- ◆ Lemon or lime wedge for garnish
- ◆ Ice

NUTRITIONAL FACTS:

- ◆ Net Carb: 19.1g
- ◆ Fiber: 0g
- ◆ Fat: 0g
- ◆ Protein: 0g
- ◆ Kcal: 175

CRAFTING THE COCKTAIL:

1. Combine all ingredients in a cocktail shaker.
2. Stir well with a cocktail spoon and pour over ice into a rocks glass.
3. Garnish with lime or lemon wedge.

INGREDIENT:

- ◆ .5 oz. fresh lime juice
- ◆ 2 oz. bourbon
- ◆ 4-6 oz. ginger beer
- ◆ Ice

NUTRITIONAL FACTS:

- ◆ Net Carb: 26g
- ◆ Fiber: 4g
- ◆ Fat: 0g
- ◆ Protein: 0g
- ◆ Kcal: 267

CRAFTING THE COCKTAIL:

1. Fill a Collins glass or a copper mug with ice.
2. Pour in the bourbon and ginger beer.

INGREDIENTS:

- ♦ 2 oz. rye whiskey, bourbon, or Canadian whiskey
- ♦ 1 oz. sweet vermouth
- ♦ 3 dashes of Angostura bitters
- ♦ Cherry for garnish
- ♦ Ice

NUTRITIONAL FACTS:

- ♦ Net Carb: 4.3g
- ♦ Fiber: .2g
- ♦ Fat: 0g
- ♦ Protein: 0g
- ♦ Kcal: 167

CRAFTING THE COCKTAIL:

1. Combine all ingredients with ice into a shaker.
2. Stir well with a cocktail spoon.
3. Strain the liquid into a chilled cocktail glass.
4. Garnish with cherry.

INGREDIENTS:

- ◆ 4-5 mint sprigs for muddling and garnish
- ◆ 2 cubes of sugar or 5 oz. simple syrup
- ◆ 2.5 oz. bourbon
- ◆ Ice

NUTRITIONAL FACTS:

- ◆ Net Carb: 6.6g
- ◆ Fiber: .2g
- ◆ Fat: 0g
- ◆ Protein: .1g
- ◆ Kcal: 199

CRAFTING THE COCKTAIL:

1. Put the sugar/simple syrup and mint in a julep cup or other cocktail glass.
2. Muddle until the mint releases its aroma.
3. Add the bourbon and stir.
4. Fill the glass with ice nd continue to stir until ice cold.
5. Garnish with mint.

INGREDIENTS:

- 1 sugar cube
- 2-3 dashes Angostura bitters
- 2 oz. rye whiskey or bourbon
- Orange peel for garnish
- Maraschino cherry to garnish
- Ice

NUTRITIONAL FACTS:

- Net Carb: 6.7g
- Fiber: .2g
- Fat: 0g
- Protein: 0g
- Kcal: 176

CRAFTING THE COCKTAIL:

1. Place the sugar cube at the bottom of an old-fashioned glass.
2. Dash the bitters over the sugar cube and muddle.
3. Fill the glass with ice and add the bourbon or whiskey.
4. Stir well.
5. Garnish with a cherry and an orange peel.

INGREDIENTS:

- ♦ 2 oz. blended scotch
- ♦ 1 oz. sweet vermouth
- ♦ 2 dashes Angostura bitters
- ♦ Orange or lemon twist to garnish
- ♦ Ice

NUTRITIONAL FACTS:

- ♦ Net Carb: 3g
- ♦ Fiber: 0g
- ♦ Fat: 0g
- ♦ Protein: 0g
- ♦ Kcal: 145

CRAFTING THE COCKTAIL:

1. Combine ice and ingredients in a shaker but do not shake.
2. Stir well.
3. Strain into a chilled cocktail glass.
4. Garnish with orange or lemon twist.

INGREDIENTS:

- ◆ 1 cube of sugar
- ◆ 1.5 oz. rye whiskey
- ◆ .25 oz. absinthe
- ◆ 3 dashes bitters
- ◆ Lemon peel to garnish
- ◆ Ice

NUTRITIONAL FACTS:

- ◆ Net Carb: 2.7g
- ◆ Fiber: 0g
- ◆ Fat: 0g
- ◆ Protein: 0g
- ◆ Kcal: 147

CRAFTING THE COCKTAIL:

1. Take an old-fashioned glass and fill it with ice.
2. Place the sugar cube and bitters n a shaker and muddle.
3. Add the whiskey and stir.
4. Empty the ice out of the glass and coat sides with absinthe
5. Pour whiskey mixture into absinthe-coated glass.
6. Garnish with the lemon peel.

INGREDIENTS:

- ◆ 1 oz. Irish whiskey
- ◆ 3 oz. water
- ◆ .25 oz. honey
- ◆ .5 oz. fresh lemon juice
- ◆ .5 oz Sriracha
- ◆ Ginger, sliced

NUTRITIONAL FACTS:

- ◆ Net Carb: 9.7g
- ◆ Fiber: .4g
- ◆ Fat: .2g
- ◆ Protein: .1g
- ◆ Kcal: 144

CRAFTING THE COCKTAIL:

1. Combine sriracha, honey, and lemon together and whisk until combined.

2. In a small pan boil the water and then add all ingredients into the pot.

3. Simmer for up to 10 minutes.

4. Pour into glass and serve.

INGREDIENTS:

- ♦ 2 oz. bourbon
- ♦ .5 oz. coffee liqueur
- ♦ 2 dashes of orange bitters
- ♦ Orange peel for garnish
- ♦ Ice

NUTRITIONAL FACTS:

- ♦ Net Carb: 9g
- ♦ Fiber: 1g
- ♦ Fat: 0g
- ♦ Protein: 0g
- ♦ Kcal: 267

CRAFTING THE COCKTAIL:

1. Add ingredients and ice into a shaker.
2. Stir until ice cold.
3. Strain into a chilled cocktail glass.
4. Flame the orange over your drink and use to garnish.

INGREDIENTS:

♦ 1.5 oz. whiskey

♦ 1.5 oz. fresh lemon juice

♦ .75 oz. simple syrup

♦ Egg white (optional)

♦ Lemon peel or maraschino cherry for garnish

♦ Ice

NUTRITIONAL FACTS:

♦ Net Carb: 13.6g

♦ Fiber: 0g

♦ Fat: 0g

♦ Protein: 0g

♦ Kcal: 162

CRAFTING THE COCKTAIL:

1. Combine all ingredients except garnishes in a cocktail shaker with ice.

2. Shake and strain the liquid into a chilled glass.

3. Garnish with a lemon peel and/or cherry.

WINE & OTHER SPIRITS

INGREDIENTS:

- ♦ 1.5 oz. Aperol
- ♦ 3 oz. Prosecco
- ♦ .75 oz. sparkling water or club soda
- ♦ Orange slice for garnish
- ♦ Ice

NUTRITIONAL FACTS:

- ♦ Net Carb: 22g
- ♦ Fiber: 0g
- ♦ Fat: 0g
- ♦ Protein: .1g
- ♦ Kcal: 210

CRAFTING THE COCKTAIL:

1. Fill a wine glass about halfway with ice cubes.
2. Add Aperol, prosecco and sparkling water.
3. Stir twice with a spoon.
4. Garnish with an orange slice.

INGREDIENTS:

- ◆ (This recipe serves 12)
- ◆ 2 cups sugar
- ◆ 1 cup water
- ◆ 3 bags frozen peaches, thawed
- ◆ 1 tsp. grated orange peel
- ◆ 4-6 (750 ml) bottles prosecco, chilled
- ◆ Orange peel twists for garnish

NUTRITIONAL FACTS:

- ◆ (1 serving)
- ◆ Net Carb: 12g
- ◆ Fiber: .4g
- ◆ Fat: 0g
- ◆ Protein: .3g
- ◆ Kcal: 130

CRAFTING THE COCKTAIL:

1. Add the water and sugar in a pan and simmer until sugar is dissolved. Let this mixture cool.

2. Puree the peaches and orange peel in a blender with 1.5 cups of simple syrup.

3. Strain through a fine mesh strainer and into a pitcher or bowl.

4. In each glass pour 2-4 tbsp. of puree and top slowly with prosecco.

5. Gently stir. Garnish with orange peel.

INGREDIENTS:

- (Serves 8)
- 1 lemongrass stalk
- 2 tbsp. fresh lemon juice
- 2 cups dry Riesling
- 2 cups fresh blood orange juice
- 6 tbsp. fresh grapefruit juice
- ¼ cup fresh lime juice
- 2 cups sparkling wine
- Blood orange wheels to garnish

NUTRITIONAL FACTS:

- Net Carb: 23.1g
- Fiber: 1.4g
- Fat: 0g
- Protein: 1g
- Kcal: 110

CRAFTING THE COCKTAIL:

1. Peel the tough exterior and muddle lemongrass and lemon juice in a pitcher.

2. Stir in Riesling and fruit juices.

3. Chill for at least 30 minutes.

4. Strain into a clean pitcher.

5. Fill wine glasses with ice and pour ¾ cups of the Sangria mixture into each glass.

6. Top with sparkling wine. Garnish with blood orange wheels.

INGREDIENTS:

- ◆ (Makes 2 ½ cups)
- ◆ 2 cups fresh blueberries
- ◆ 1 wide strip of lemon zest
- ◆ 2 cups applejack brandy
- ◆ Simple syrup (for serving)
- ◆ Sparkling wine or club soda (optional for serving)

NUTRITIONAL FACTS:

- ◆ (1 serving)
- ◆ Net Carb: 47.9
- ◆ Fiber: 7.1g
- ◆ Fat: 1g
- ◆ Protein: 2.2g
- ◆ Kcal: 327

CRAFTING THE COCKTAIL:

1. Combine blueberries, lemon zest, and brandy in a jar and seal tightly.

2. Let sit in dark and cool place daily.

3. When the mixture is deep purple the drink is ready to serve.

4. When it is ready, strain mixture through a cheesecloth into a pitcher or large bowl.

5. Slowly add pours of simple syrup to taste.

6. Chill until cold and then sere in cordial glasses.

INGREDIENTS:

- ♦ 2 oz. silver tequila
- ♦ .5 oz Grand Marnier
- ♦ .5 oz. fresh lime juice
- ♦ .5 oz. fresh lemon juice
- ♦ 1.5 oz. ghost chili simple syrup
- ♦ Ground chili to rim glass
- ♦ Salt to rim glass
- ♦ Lime wheels to garnish
- ♦ Ice

NUTRITIONAL FACTS:

- ♦ Net Carb: 28g
- ♦ Fiber: .2g
- ♦ Fat: 0g
- ♦ Protein: .2g
- ♦ Kcal: 228

CRAFTING THE COCKTAIL:

1. Make ghost pepper simple syrup.

2. Pour salt and ground chili onto a plate. Mix thoroughly.

3. Moisten glass rims with limes and roll rim in the salt/chili mixture.

4. Combine ice and all ingredients in a shaker.

5. Shake well and strain over ice into a rocks glass.

6. Garnish with a lime wheel.

INGREDIENTS:

- ◆ 2 oz. brandy
- ◆ 1 oz. sweet vermouth
- ◆ ½ tsp simple syrup
- ◆ 2 dashes Angostura bitters
- ◆ Cherry to garnish
- ◆ Ice

NUTRITIONAL FACTS:

- ◆ Net Carb: 4g
- ◆ Fiber: 0g
- ◆ Fat: 0g
- ◆ Protein: 0g
- ◆ Kcal: 191

CRAFTING THE COCKTAIL:

1. Combine all the ingredients in a cocktail shaker with ice.
2. Shake well.
3. Strain into a chilled cocktail glass.
4. Garnish with a cherry.

INGREDIENTS:

- ♦ 3 oz. green tea
- ♦ 1.5 oz. tequila
- ♦ 1 oz. Chinese 5-spice syrup
- ♦ .25 oz. fresh lemon juice
- ♦ 1.5 oz dark beer
- ♦ Orange peel for garnish

NUTRITIONAL FACTS:

- ♦ Net Carb: 43g
- ♦ Fiber: 4g
- ♦ Fat: 2g
- ♦ Protein: 7g
- ♦ Kcal: 335

CRAFTING THE COCKTAIL:

1. Combine all ingredients in a cocktail shaker but do not shake.
2. Stir the mixture with a cocktail spoon.
3. Fill a glass with ice and pour the mixture over.
4. Garnish with a heated orange peel.

INGREDIENTS:

- ♦ 4 oz. dry prosecco or sparkling white wine
- ♦ 1 oz. sweet vermouth
- ♦ .5 oz. Campari
- ♦ Club soda
- ♦ Lime wheel for garnish

NUTRITIONAL FACTS:

- ♦ Net Carbs: 300g
- ♦ Fiber: 0g
- ♦ Fat: 0g
- ♦ Protein: 0g
- ♦ Kcal: 166

CRAFTING THE COCKTAIL:

1. Pour wine into an ice-filled glass.
2. Add the vermouth and Campari.
3. Top with club soda and stir.
4. Garnish with a lime wheel.

INGREDIENTS:

- ◆ 1 tsp. white sugar
- ◆ 2 oz. Cognac
- ◆ 1 oz. orange liqueur
- ◆ .5 oz, fresh lemon juice
- ◆ Ice

NUTRITIONAL FACTS:

- ◆ Net Carbs: 4.1 g
- ◆ Fiber: .1g
- ◆ Fat: 0g
- ◆ Protein: .1g
- ◆ Kcal: 282

CRAFTING THE COCKTAIL:

1. Pour sugar onto a plate, lightly wet the glass rims and dip the glass into sugar.

2. Chill glass.

3. Combine all the ingredients and ice into a shaker.

4. Shake and strain the liquid into the chilled, sugar-rimmed glass.

INGREDIENTS:

- ◆ 1.5 oz. tequila
- ◆ .75 oz. Porto
- ◆ .75 oz. Cherry Heering
- ◆ .75 oz. fresh orange juice
- ◆ *black citrus foam
- ◆ 4 oz. simple syrup
- ◆ 4 oz. lemon juice
- ◆ 4 tbs. activated charcoal
- ◆ 4 egg whites

NUTRITIONAL FACTS:

- ◆ Net Carbs: 2.5g
- ◆ Fiber: .1g
- ◆ Fat: .1g
- ◆ Protein: 3.7g
- ◆ Kcal: 268

CRAFTING THE COCKTAIL:

Black Citrus foam:

1. Add all ingredients into a stainless whipped cream dispenser.

2. Shake well and charge twice.

3. Dispense on top of each cocktail.

Cocktail:

1. Add all ingredients and ice into shaker.

2. Shake and strain the liquid into a chilled glass.

3. Top with black citrus foam.

INGREDIENTS:

- ◆ 2 oz. absinthe
- ◆ 1 oz. brandy
- ◆ .5 oz. gin
- ◆ 3 oz. vodka
- ◆ 1 oz. Crème de Mures

NUTRITIONAL FACTS:

- ◆ Net Carbs: 11g
- ◆ Fiber: 0g
- ◆ Fat: 0g
- ◆ Protein: 0g
- ◆ Kcal: 499

CRAFTING THE COCKTAIL:

1. Combine all ingredients in a cocktail shaker with ice but do not shake.

2. Stir well until very cold and then strain the liquid into a chilled glass.

INGREDIENTS:

- ◆ 1 oz. brandy
- ◆ 1 oz. light rum
- ◆ 1 oz. triple sec
- ◆ .5 oz. fresh lemon juice
- ◆ Lemon twist to garnish
- ◆ Ice

NUTRITIONAL FACTS:

- ◆ Net carbs: 23g
- ◆ Fiber: 1g
- ◆ Fat: 0g
- ◆ Protein: 3g
- ◆ Kcal: 211

CRAFTING THE COCKTAIL:

1. Combine ice and all the ingredients into a shaker.

2. Shake well.

3. Strain into a chilled cocktail glass.

4. Garnish with the lemon twist.

INGREDIENTS:

- ♦ 2 oz. brewed espresso
- ♦ 1 oz. bourbon
- ♦ .5 oz. Cognac
- ♦ 1 large scoop of ice cream

NUTRITIONAL FACTS:

- ♦ Net Carbs: 73g
- ♦ Fiber: 2g
- ♦ Fat: 7g
- ♦ Protein: 5g
- ♦ Kcal: 458

CRAFTING THE COCKTAIL:

1. Combine espresso, Cognac and bourbon in a cup.

2. Scoop ice cream into a small glass and pour mixture over ice cream.

INGREDIENTS:

- ♦ (Serves 30)
- ♦ 12 lemons
- ♦ 2 cups light raw sugar
- ♦ 1 750ml bottle Cognac
- ♦ 1 750ml bottle bourbon
- ♦ 1 750ml bottle rum
- ♦ 3 750ml bottles of chilled, sparkling wine
- ♦ 5 lbs. ice

NUTRITIONAL FACTS:

- ♦ Net Carbs: 7.8g
- ♦ Fiber: .2g
- ♦ Fat: 0g
- ♦ Protein: .1g
- ♦ Kcal: 360

CRAFTING THE COCKTAIL:

1. Peel all the lemon rind making sure to not get any of the bitter pith.

2. Place peels in a large bowl and add the sugar.

3. Muddle the two until the oils are released from the lemon peels. Let sit for at least half an hour.

4. Take the remaining lemons and juice them. Once the peels have set add the lemon juice to the bowl.

5. Stir until the sugar dissolves, then strain into a jug or bottle.

6. Add water, shake the mixture and chill until you are ready to finish the punch.

7. When ready take out your large punch bowl and fill with ice.

8. Combine lemon/sugar mixture with the bottles of liquor and stir to combine.

INGREDIENTS:

- 1.5 oz. whiskey
- .5 oz. Cherry brandy
- Maraschino cherry to garnish
- Ice

NUTRITIONAL FACTS:

- Net Carbs: 2g
- Fiber: 0g
- Fat: 0g
- Protein: 0g
- Kcal: 115

CRAFTING THE COCKTAIL:

1. Combine whiskey and brandy with ice in a shaker.

2. Stir with a cocktail spoon and pour over ice into a glass.

3. Garnish with a cherry.

INGREDIENTS:

- ◆ 1 sugar cube
- ◆ 1 dash of Angostura bitters
- ◆ 2 oz. Cognac
- ◆ 2 oz. Champagne
- ◆ .25 oz. Chartreuse liqueur

NUTRITIONAL FACTS:

- ◆ Net Carbs: 0g
- ◆ Fiber: 0g
- ◆ Fat: 0g
- ◆ Protein: 0g
- ◆ Kcal: 233

CRAFTING THE COCKTAIL:

1. Place sugar cube in a shaker and soak with angostura bitters.
2. Add ice and Cognac to the mixture and stir well
3. Pour into glass. Top with Champagne.
4. Drizzle Chartreuse on top and then fill the glass with ice.

INGREDIENTS:

- ◆ .5 oz. triple sec
- ◆ .5 oz. light rum
- ◆ .5 oz. gin
- ◆ .5 oz. vodka
- ◆ .5 oz. tequila
- ◆ 2 oz. cola
- ◆ 1 oz. sour mix
- ◆ Lemon wedge to garnish

NUTRITIONAL FACTS:

- ◆ Net Carbs: 43g
- ◆ Fiber: 4g
- ◆ Fat: 2g
- ◆ Protein: 7g
- ◆ Kcal: 335

CRAFTING THE COCKTAIL:

1. Combine all alcohol and the sour mix in a cocktail shaker with ice.

2. Stir well with a cocktail spoon.

3. Add ice to a Collins glass. Pour the mixture over the ice and then top with cola.

4. Garnish with a lemon wedge.

INGREDIENTS:

- ◆ 2 oz. rye whiskey
- ◆ .75 oz. sweet vermouth
- ◆ 2 tsps. Cherry Heering
- ◆ ½ tsp. absinthe
- ◆ Cherry for garnish

NUTRITIONAL FACTS:

- ◆ Net Carbs: 0g
- ◆ Fiber: 0g
- ◆ Fat: 0g
- ◆ Protein: 0g
- ◆ Kcal: 318

CRAFTING THE COCKTAIL:

1. Combine all the ingredients in a cocktail shaker with ice.
2. Stir with cocktail spoon until cold.
3. Pour into a chilled cocktail glass.
4. Garnish with a cherry.

INGREDIENTS:

- ◆ 2 oz. vodka
- ◆ 2 oz. gin
- ◆ 4 oz. pink grapefruit juice
- ◆ 4 sprigs of fresh thyme
- ◆ Dry Rose champagne to top off
- ◆ 1.5 oz. elderflower liqueur

NUTRITIONAL FACTS:

- ◆ Net Carbs: 12.3g
- ◆ Fiber: 0g
- ◆ Fat: 0g
- ◆ Protein: .5g
- ◆ Kcal: 360.5

CRAFTING THE COCKTAIL:

1. Combine vodka, gin, grapefruit juice and 2 sprigs of time with ice in a shaker.

2. Shake until very cold and then strain into a chilled cocktail glass.

3. Top with champagne.

4. Garnish with the remaining thyme.

INGREDIENTS:

- ◆ 2 oz. white rum
- ◆ .5 oz. sherry
- ◆ .5 oz Amontillado
- ◆ .75 oz. passion fruit puree
- ◆ .5 oz. hibiscus infused simple syrup
- ◆ Mint to garnish
- ◆ .5 oz fresh lemon juice

NUTRITIONAL FACTS:

- ◆ Net Carbs: 21.3g
- ◆ Fiber: .3g
- ◆ Fat: 0g
- ◆ Protein: .1g
- ◆ Kcal: 224

CRAFTING THE COCKTAIL:

1. Combine all ingredient with ice in a shaker.

2. Shake and then strain the liquid into a chilled cocktail glass.

3. Garnish with mint.

INGREDIENTS:

- ◆ 3 oz. tequila
- ◆ 1 oz. light rum
- ◆ 1 oz. dark rum
- ◆ .5 oz fresh lemon juice
- ◆ .5 oz fresh lime juice
- ◆ 1 tsp. sugar
- ◆ 2 oz. ale

NUTRITIONAL FACTS:

- ◆ Net Carbs: 8.6g
- ◆ Fiber: .2g
- ◆ Fat: 0g
- ◆ Protein: .4g
- ◆ Kcal: 369

CRAFTING THE COCKTAIL:

1. Combine all ingredients except ale in a shaker half-filled with ice.
2. Shake well until ice cold.
3. Strain liquid into a Collins glass filled with ice.
4. Top with ale.

VIEUX CARRE

INGREDIENTS:
- .75 oz. rye whiskey
- .75 oz. Cognac
- .75 oz. sweet vermouth
- ½ tsp. Benedictine liqueur
- 1 dash of Peychaud's bitters
- 1 dash Angostura bitters
- Cherry to garnish
- Ice

NUTRITIONAL FACTS:
- Net Carbs: 10g
- Fiber: 0g
- Fat: 1g
- Protein: 0g
- Kcal: 221

CRAFTING THE COCKTAIL:
1. Combine ingredients with ice in a shaker.
2. Stir with a cocktail spoon until ice cold.
3. Strain the liquid into an old-fashioned glass filled with ice.
4. Garnish with a cherry.

INGREDIENTS:

- ◆ 5 oz. green tea, chilled
- ◆ .5 oz. coconut milk
- ◆ 5 oz. coconut soda, chilled

NUTRITIONAL FACTS:

- ◆ Net Carbs: 2g
- ◆ Fiber: 0g
- ◆ Fat: 2.5g
- ◆ Protein: .5g
- ◆ Kcal: 30

CRAFTING THE MOCKTAIL:

1. Brew green tea and chill.
2. Combine green tea and coconut milk.
3. Pour the liquid in a tall highball glass.
4. Top glass off with chilled soda.

INGREDIENTS:

- ◆ **(Makes 3 liters)**
- ◆ 1.5 cups lemon juice
- ◆ 1 ¾ cups sugar
- ◆ 8 cups of coconut water
- ◆ 4 cups water
- ◆ Simple syrup infused with lavender to taste
- ◆ Lemon slices for garnish

NUTRITIONAL FACTS:

- ◆ **(8 oz. serving)**
- ◆ Net Carbs: 24.5g
- ◆ Fiber: .1g
- ◆ Fat: 0g
- ◆ Protein: .5g
- ◆ Kcal: 93

CRAFTING THE MOCKTAIL:

1. In a pitcher mix the sugar, lemon juice, water, and coconut water.

2. Stir together until the sugar dissolves.

3. Then slowly add lavender simple syrup stirring while doing this until the lemonade is to your taste.

4. Pour into ice-filled glasses and garnish with lemon slices.

INGREDIENTS:

- ◆ 10 mint leaves
- ◆ .5 oz. simple syrup
- ◆ 3 oz. cold brew coffee or tea
- ◆ 10mg CBD lavender bitters (optional)

NUTRITIONAL FACTS:

- ◆ Net Carbs: 103g
- ◆ Fiber: 0g
- ◆ Fat: 2.5g
- ◆ Protein: 5g
- ◆ Kcal: 455

CRAFTING THE MOCKTAIL:

1. Muddle half of the mint in a shaker.

2. Combine cold brew, simple syrup, and lavender bitters (optional) in a cocktail shaker with ice.

3. Stir with a cocktail spoon until ice cold.

4. Strain into an ice-filled glass and garnish with remaining mint.

INGREDIENTS:

- ◆ **(Makes 1 pitcher)**
- ◆ 1 grapefruit for juice and garnish
- ◆ 2 cups ice
- ◆ 3 12 oz. cans ginger beer
- ◆ A handful of basil for garnish
- ◆ ¼ cup basil-infused simple syrup

NUTRITIONAL FACTS:

- ◆ **(8 oz. serving)**
- ◆ Net Carb: 14.3g
- ◆ Fiber: 0g
- ◆ Fat: 0g
- ◆ Protein: .2g
- ◆ Kcal: 58

CRAFTING THE MOCKTAIL:

1. Juice one grapefruit and segment grapefruit slices for later garnishing.

2. Fill pitcher half full of ice.

3. Combine all the ingredient into a pitcher.

4. Mix well.

5. Garnish with grapefruit segments and basil.

INGREDIENTS:

- ◆ 1 12 oz. can of Dr. Pepper
- ◆ 2 oz. coconut syrup
- ◆ 1 lime freshly squeezed
- ◆ Crushed ice

NUTRITIONAL FACTS:

- ◆ Net Carb: 89.7g
- ◆ Fiber: .2g
- ◆ Fat: 0g
- ◆ Protein: .2g
- ◆ Kcal: 351

CRAFTING THE MOCKTAIL:

1. Fill glass with crushed ice.

2. Pour all ingredients over ice.

3. Stir well and drink.

IMPRINT

Printed in Great Britain
by Amazon